JORDAN TRAVEL GUIDE 2024 UPDATED

Discover the Hidden Treasures of Jordan: An Insider's Guide to Ancient Ruins, Desert Adventures, Timeless Traditions, and Culinary Delights

Harrison wells

WELCOME TO JORDAN

Welcome to the enchanting land of Jordan, a country steeped in history, culture, and natural beauty. Have you ever wondered about the fascinating fact that Jordan is home to one of the New Seven Wonders of the World? The ancient city of Petra, carved into rose-red cliffs over 2,000 years ago, is a testament to the architectural brilliance of the Nabateans and a must-see marvel for any traveler. Nestled in the heart of the Middle East,

Jordan offers a diverse tapestry of experiences, from exploring ancient ruins and wandering through vibrant markets to soaking in the therapeutic waters of the Dead Sea and venturing into the otherworldly landscapes of Wadi Rum.

As you delve deeper into Jordan's rich tapestry, you'll discover a land of contrasts and contradictions. From the bustling streets of Amman, the capital city, where modernity meets tradition, to the serene desert landscapes of Wadi Rum, where time seems to stand still, Jordan offers a diverse array of experiences for every traveler.

One cannot visit Jordan without experiencing the warm embrace of its people. The Jordanian hospitality, known locally as "Jameed," is legendary, and you'll find it woven into every interaction, from sharing a cup of sweet mint tea with locals to exploring ancient ruins with knowledgeable guides who are eager to share the stories of their ancestors.

While Petra stands as a beacon of Jordan's ancient heritage, the country's natural wonders are equally enthralling. The Dead Sea, renowned for its therapeutic properties and the sensation of effortlessly floating on its buoyant waters, is a surreal experience that leaves a lasting impression. And let's not forget the stunning landscapes of Wadi

Rum, with its towering sandstone mountains and vast, moon-like deserts, offering a backdrop that has captivated filmmakers and explorers alike.

As you embark on your journey through Jordan, you'll also have the opportunity to savor its delectable cuisine. From succulent grilled meats and fragrant rice dishes to mezze spreads bursting with flavors, Jordanian cuisine is a tantalizing fusion of Middle Eastern traditions and local specialties.

Whether you're an avid history buff, a nature enthusiast, or simply seeking a unique and memorable travel experience, Jordan has something to offer for everyone. So, are you ready to immerse yourself in the wonders of this captivating country?

HISTORY OF JORDAN

Jordan, nestled in the heart of the Middle East, boasts a history that spans millennia. Its strategic location has made it a crossroads of civilizations and a witness to the rise and fall of empires.

The earliest traces of human habitation in what is now Jordan date back to the Paleolithic period, with evidence of nomadic hunter-gatherer communities. By the Neolithic era, around 7500 BCE, settled agricultural communities began to emerge, cultivating crops and raising livestock in the fertile Jordan Valley.

In antiquity, Jordan was home to several powerful kingdoms. The region known as Transjordan formed part of the biblical lands of Ammon, Moab, and Edom. These ancient kingdoms are mentioned in the Hebrew Bible, with significant historical and cultural significance.

Around the 8th century BCE, the Assyrians established dominance over the area, followed by the Babylonians, Persians, and eventually, the Hellenistic Seleucids. The city of Petra, capital of the Nabatean Kingdom, became a thriving center of trade and culture, attaining its zenith in the 4th century BCE.

In 63 BCE, the Roman Empire conquered the region, incorporating it into the province of Arabia Petraea. The Byzantine period saw the spread of Christianity, with Jordan becoming home to numerous churches, monasteries, and pilgrim sites, including the baptism site of Jesus at Bethany Beyond the Jordan.

The 7th century brought the advent of Islam, with the Islamic Caliphate swiftly expanding its influence across the Arabian Peninsula, including present-day Jordan. The Umayyad Caliphate established its administrative center in Damascus, exerting control over the region.

The Crusaders made their mark on Jordan during the 12th and 13th centuries, leaving behind formidable fortresses like Kerak and Montreal, which still stand today as testament to their presence.

By the 16th century, the Ottoman Empire extended its dominion over the area, ruling for over four centuries. During this time, the Ottomans left an indelible mark on Jordan's architectural and cultural heritage.

Following the disintegration of the Ottoman Empire after World War I, the League of Nations granted

Britain the mandate to govern the area. In 1946, Transjordan gained independence, becoming the Hashemite Kingdom of Jordan under King Abdullah I.

Over the decades, Jordan has played a pivotal role in regional affairs, including the Arab-Israeli conflict, hosting waves of refugees, and actively pursuing peace and stability in the Middle East.

DISCOVERING JORDAN

Amman.

Amman, the capital city of Jordan, is a vibrant and historically rich metropolis nestled in the heart of the Middle East. With a history dating back thousands of years, it has evolved from ancient settlements to a bustling modern city while still retaining its unique cultural heritage.

The cityscape of Amman is a juxtaposition of old and new. On one hand, you have the bustling downtown area, known as Al-Balad, which houses the historic Roman Theater and the Citadel, two iconic archaeological sites. The Roman Theater, with a seating capacity of over 6,000, is a testament to the city's ancient past, while the Citadel, perched on Jabal Al-Qala'a, offers panoramic views of the city and contains various ruins and artifacts from different historical periods.

As you move through the city, you'll encounter a blend of architectural styles, reflecting the various influences that have shaped Amman over the centuries. From the narrow, winding streets of the older neighborhoods to the modern skyscrapers that dot the skyline, the city offers a visual tapestry that tells the story of its evolution.

Amman is also a hub of culture and commerce. The city's markets and souks are a bustling hive of activity, where locals and visitors alike can browse through a wide array of goods, from traditional handicrafts and spices to modern fashion and electronics. The vibrant street food scene is a testament to Jordan's culinary heritage, offering a diverse range of flavors and dishes that cater to various tastes.

Education and innovation thrive in Amman, with numerous universities, research institutions, and tech startups contributing to the city's intellectual landscape. The King Abdullah II Street, often referred to as the "Technology Street," is a testament to the city's commitment to modernization and technological advancement.

Amman's neighborhoods are a microcosm of its diverse population. From the affluent areas of Abdoun and Sweifieh, where you'll find high-end boutiques and restaurants, to the more traditional neighborhoods like Jabal Amman and Jabal Al-Weibdeh, each district offers its own unique atmosphere and character.

Finally, Amman's strategic location makes it an ideal base for exploring the wider wonders of Jordan. From the ancient city of Petra to the dramatic landscapes of Wadi Rum, the historical sites of Jerash, and the serene shores of the Dead Sea, Amman serves as a gateway to the rich tapestry o

The Citadel (Jabal al-Qal'a):

History: The Citadel, perched on a hill in the heart of Amman, boasts a history spanning thousands of years. It was first established as a Bronze Age fortress around 1800 BCE. Later, during the Roman period, it became the city of Philadelphia, and then served as a Umayyad palace complex.

Facts: The most iconic feature is the Temple of Hercules, which once housed a massive statue of the mythical hero. The ruins of the temple still stand, and from the Citadel, visitors can enjoy breathtaking panoramic views of Amman.

Roman Theater:

History: Constructed during the reign of Emperor Antoninus Pius (138-161 AD), the Roman Theater is an architectural marvel from the Roman era. It was used for various performances, including dramas, poetry readings, and other public events.

Facts: With a seating capacity of approximately 6,000 spectators, it was one of the largest and most well-preserved Roman theaters in the ancient world.

Amman Citadel Archaeological Museum:

History: Housed within the Citadel, this museum is a treasure trove of artifacts that reflect the rich history of the site. It encompasses relics from the Bronze Age, Roman, Byzantine, and Islamic periods, providing a comprehensive view of the diverse civilizations that inhabited the area.

Facts: The museum offers valuable insights into the cultural, architectural, and artistic achievements of the various historical periods in Jordan.

King Abdullah I Mosque:

History: Constructed between 1982 and 1989, the King Abdullah I Mosque is a modern architectural masterpiece named in honor of Jordan's first king, King Abdullah I.

Facts: Its distinctive blue dome and towering minaret are prominent features of Amman's skyline. The mosque's prayer hall can accommodate up to 7,000 worshippers.

Rainbow Street (Jabal Amman):

History: Rainbow Street, nestled in the historic Jabal Amman neighborhood, has been a cultural and entertainment hub for decades. It has witnessed the evolution of Amman's social scene.

Facts: Today, it is known for its trendy shops, art galleries, and vibrant nightlife, making it a must-visit destination for those seeking a blend of modern and traditional Jordanian culture.

Jordan Museum:

History: Established in 2014, the Jordan Museum is a modern institution that showcases Jordan's rich cultural heritage. It houses artifacts from various archaeological sites around the country, representing a wide range of historical periods.

Facts: One of the most notable exhibits is the collection of the Dead Sea Scrolls, which are ancient manuscripts of great historical and religious significance.

Amman Roman Nymphaeum:

History: This ornate public fountain was built in the 2nd century AD and served as a crucial water source for the city of Philadelphia (Amman during the Roman period).

Facts: The Nymphaeum is adorned with intricate carvings and dedicatory inscriptions. It was dedicated to the nymphs, who were considered protectors of springs in Roman mythology.

The Jordan Folklore Museum:

History: Situated near the Roman Theater, this museum is a tribute to Jordanian heritage. It showcases traditional clothing, musical instruments, household items, and other artifacts that provide a window into the daily life and customs of Jordanian people throughout history.

The Duke's Diwan (Diwan al-Majlis):

History: Dating back to the Umayyad period, this historical site served as a governmental meeting place during ancient times.

Facts: Today, it houses the Jordan Museum of Popular Tradition, which features displays of traditional Jordanian crafts, along with artifacts that offer a glimpse into the rich cultural tapestry of the region.

The Hashemite Plaza:

History: Named after the Hashemite monarchy, this central plaza is a bustling hub of activity and a popular gathering place for both locals and tourists.

Facts: The Hashemite Plaza often hosts events, celebrations, and cultural festivals, adding a lively touch to Amman's social scene.

Souk Jara:

History: Located in the heart of Jabal Amman, Souk Jara is a vibrant open-air market that operates during the summer months. It continues a long tradition of markets in the area.

Facts: Visitors can explore a wide range of handmade crafts, clothing, jewelry, and indulge in delicious street food, offering a taste of Jordanian craftsmanship and culinary delights.

The Royal Automobile Museum:

History: Established in 2003, this museum provides a unique perspective on Jordan's royal family through their extensive collection of cars, many of which were used in historical events and ceremonies.

Facts: It showcases a diverse array of vehicles, offering a fascinating glimpse into the modern history of Jordan and its royal legacy.

Wild Jordan Center:

History: This eco-friendly center was established to promote sustainable tourism and support local communities. It is dedicated to preserving Jordan's natural heritage.

Facts: The Wild Jordan Center offers a range of products made by local artisans and serves as an educational hub for visitors interested in learning about Jordan's diverse ecosystems and conservation efforts.

Aqaba

Aqaba, located at the southern tip of Jordan, is a coastal gem on the Red Sea. This port city boasts a rich history, with archaeological sites like Ayla showcasing its ancient roots. Aqaba's strategic location has made it a crucial trading hub for centuries.

The city's natural beauty is a major draw. The Red Sea's crystal-clear waters and vibrant coral reefs make it a paradise for snorkelers and divers. Aqaba also offers a range of water activities, from sailing to jet-skiing, ensuring there's something for every water enthusiast.

Aqaba's skyline is punctuated by modern hotels and resorts, providing visitors with luxurious accommodations and stunning sea views. The city's hospitality sector has flourished, offering a diverse range of dining options, from local Jordanian cuisine to international fare.

Beyond the shores, Aqaba's surrounding deserts provide opportunities for adventure seekers. Jeep tours, camel treks, and hiking trails lead to breathtaking vistas and ancient archaeological sites, including the fabled city of Petra, a few hours' drive away.

Aqaba Archaeological Museum:

Facts: The museum's collection includes pottery, jewelry, coins, and inscriptions from various historical periods. Notable exhibits feature artifacts from the Bronze Age settlement of Tell el-Khleifeh, showcasing Aqaba's ancient roots as a trading hub. Visitors can also see items from the Islamic and Ottoman eras, providing a comprehensive view of the city's evolution.

Aqaba Castle (Mamluk Castle):

Facts: The castle's strategic location allowed it to control trade routes and protect against potential maritime invasions. Its architectural design, characterized by thick stone walls and watchtowers, exemplifies Mamluk defensive architecture. The castle's well-preserved state provides a tangible link to the region's historical military significance.

Aqaba Marine Park:

Facts: The marine park encompasses a diverse range of marine ecosystems, including seagrass beds, mangrove forests, and coral reefs. These habitats support a remarkable variety of marine life, including over 100 species of fish and numerous invertebrates. The park's conservation efforts have contributed to the ongoing protection of the Red Sea's fragile ecosystem.

South Beach:

Facts: South Beach has become a thriving hub for water sports enthusiasts. Visitors can partake in thrilling activities such as kiteboarding and paddleboarding, making it an ideal destination for adventure seekers. The beach's soft sands and clear, calm waters also create a perfect environment for sunbathing and relaxation.

Aqaba Aquarium:

Facts: The aquarium's exhibits not only showcase Red Sea marine life but also serve an educational purpose. Interactive displays and informative panels provide insights into the biology and behavior of various species. The aquarium's conservation efforts play a vital role in promoting awareness about the importance of protecting marine environments.

Lawrence's Spring:

Facts: The spring's location in the arid desert landscape is a testament to its historical significance as a crucial water source for both travelers and local wildlife. The spring's association with T.E. Lawrence adds an extra layer of historical intrigue, offering visitors a tangible link to the region's role in the Arab Revolt.

Bertha's Mosque:

Facts: The mosque's architectural features, including its distinctive dome and geometric patterns, exemplify early Islamic design. Its location in Aqaba underscores the city's historical importance as a center of trade and cultural exchange. The mosque stands as a tangible testament to Aqaba's rich Islamic heritage.

Aqaba Bird Observatory:

Facts: The observatory's location along migratory bird routes has established it as a vital research center. Birdwatching enthusiasts can witness a diverse array of avian species, including raptors, waterfowl, and songbirds. The observatory's educational programs and research initiatives contribute to the conservation of Jordan's avian biodiversity.

Tala Bay Resort:

Facts: Tala Bay's development has transformed the coastline into a premier leisure destination. The resort's luxurious accommodations, world-class dining, and array of recreational activities make it a sought-after destination for travelers seeking both relaxation and adventure.

Ayla Oasis Development Project:

Facts: The Ayla project's scope extends beyond tourism, aiming to create a sustainable, integrated community. Its marinas, golf courses, and cultural venues contribute to Aqaba's transformation into a dynamic, world-class destination for both residents and visitors alike.

Palm Beach Aqaba:

Facts: The beach's clear, shallow waters make it an ideal location for snorkeling and observing vibrant marine life. Its tranquil ambiance and picturesque setting offer visitors a peaceful escape from the bustling city, making it a popular spot for both locals and tourists.

Aqaba Fort (Mamluk Fort):

Facts: The fort's elevated position allows for stunning panoramic views of Aqaba and its coastline. Its well-preserved state invites visitors to explore the structure's architectural details and imagine the historical events that transpired within its walls.

The Royal Yacht Club:

Facts: The club's vibrant maritime community fosters a love for boating and water-based activities. Sailing events, regattas, and yacht races are a regular feature, attracting sailing enthusiasts from around the world.

Diving in Aqaba:

Facts: Aqaba's marine life is renowned for its biodiversity, with over 400 species of coral and an array of marine creatures inhabiting the Red Sea's depths. Divers can explore fascinating underwater landscapes, including coral gardens, submerged wrecks, and captivating underwater caves.

Aqaba Flagpole:

Facts: Standing tall as one of the world's tallest flagpoles, the Aqaba Flagpole is a symbol of national pride and unity. Its towering presence along the coastline serves as a visual landmark, emphasizing Jordan's cultural and historical significance.

Irbid

Irbid, located in the north of Jordan, is the country's second-largest city and a hub of education and culture. Home to several prominent universities, including Yarmouk University, it has earned the nickname "The City of Knowledge". This academic influence has contributed to Irbid's dynamic and youthful atmosphere.

The city's historical roots run deep, with archaeological sites like Tell Irbid revealing evidence of ancient settlements dating back thousands of years. The Ottoman-era Ajloun Castle, situated in the nearby Ajloun Governorate, is a prominent historical landmark.

Irbid's vibrant markets and commercial districts offer a diverse range of goods and services, from traditional souks to modern shopping centers. The city's culinary scene showcases a blend of Jordanian and international flavors, making it a gastronomic delight for visitors.

Surrounded by picturesque countryside and fertile farmland, Irbid enjoys a relatively temperate climate, making it an attractive destination for those seeking a break from the hustle and bustle of larger cities. The nearby Yarmouk Nature Reserve offers opportunities for hiking and bird-watching amidst stunning natural landscapes.

Yarmouk University:

Facts: Yarmouk University, nestled near the Yarmouk River, boasts a sprawling campus adorned with picturesque views and lush green spaces. With a diverse student body and a wide array of academic programs, it stands as a cornerstone of higher education in Jordan. Since its establishment in 1976, it has been a hub for intellectual growth, research, and innovation.

Umm Qais (Gadara):

Facts: Once known as Gadara in the ancient world, Umm Qais is an archaeological treasure trove located just a short distance from Irbid. The site unravels the stories of bygone eras through its impeccably preserved ruins. Visitors can marvel at a Roman theater, walk along colonnaded streets, and explore Byzantine churches. Moreover, the breathtaking views encompassing the Sea of Galilee, Golan Heights, and the Jordan Valley make a visit to Umm Qais an unforgettable experience.

Ajloun Castle:

Facts: While not situated directly in Irbid, Ajloun Castle is a historic gem worth the short journey. Constructed by the Ayyubids in the 12th century, the castle's purpose was to fortify the region against potential Crusader incursions. The architectural marvel showcases the mastery of Islamic military design and offers panoramic vistas that extend over the surrounding countryside.

Jordan Museum of Natural History:

Facts: As an integral part of Yarmouk University, the Jordan Museum of Natural History is a treasure trove of geological, botanical, and zoological wonders. Established in 2006, this institution houses extensive collections of fossils, minerals, plants, and native Jordanian wildlife. It stands as a valuable resource for students, researchers, and nature enthusiasts alike.

Arabella Mall:

Facts: Arabella Mall is a contemporary shopping complex in Irbid, where visitors can indulge in a diverse retail experience. Beyond its plethora of international and local brands, the mall boasts an array of restaurants, a cinema for entertainment, and a dedicated play area for children. Arabella Mall has quickly become a go-to destination for both shopping enthusiasts and families seeking leisurely activities.

Yarmouk Cultural Center:

Facts: Serving as a vibrant hub for cultural exchange and expression, the Yarmouk Cultural Center in Irbid is a beacon for artists and cultural enthusiasts. The center is renowned for hosting a wide range of exhibitions, workshops, and captivating performances. Its mission is to foster local talent and cultivate a strong sense of community through creative endeavors.

Martyr's Memorial and Museum:

Facts: This museum is a poignant tribute to the Jordanian soldiers who made the ultimate sacrifice in service to their nation. Through a collection of photographs, artifacts, and documents, the museum vividly chronicles Jordan's military history. It stands as a testament to the indomitable spirit and unwavering dedication of those who have served their country.

Irbid Archaeological Museum:

Facts: Established in 1986, the Irbid Archaeological Museum is a treasure trove of historical artifacts from various periods, including the Bronze Age, Iron Age, Roman, and Byzantine eras. It offers invaluable insights into the ancient civilizations that once flourished in the region, providing a tangible link to the past.

Al Hassan Industrial Estate:

Facts: The Al Hassan Industrial Estate plays a pivotal role in Irbid's economic landscape. Hosting a diverse range of industries, including manufacturing, production, and technology, it contributes significantly to the city's industrial development. The estate stands as a testament to Irbid's growth and prosperity.

Irbid National University:

Facts: Established in 1994, Irbid National University has emerged as a distinguished institution of higher education in the city.

Renowned for its focus on research and innovation, the university offers a diverse range of academic programs. It has played a pivotal role in shaping the intellectual and educational landscape of Irbid.

Al Sharee'ah Mosque:

Facts: Al Sharee'ah Mosque is a cherished symbol of religious and communal significance in Irbid. Its architectural design, characterized by traditional Islamic styles, reflects the city's deep-rooted cultural heritage. The mosque continues to serve as a place of worship and a gathering point for the local community.

Princess Basma Public Park:

Facts: Named after Princess Basma, a member of the Jordanian royal family, this park has been a beloved recreational space for residents of Irbid for years. With its lush greenery, tranquil fountains, walking paths, play areas, and spaces for picnics, it provides a serene escape from the urban hustle and bustle.

Irbid City Centre:

Facts: Irbid City Centre stands as a modern shopping and entertainment complex catering to the needs and desires of residents and visitors alike.

The mall is a bustling hub of activity, offering a diverse array of shops, restaurants, a cinema, and recreational facilities. It has become a popular destination for shopping, dining, and leisure activities in Irbid.

King Abdullah University Hospital:

Facts: Affiliated with Jordan University of Science and Technology, King Abdullah University Hospital has been a beacon of comprehensive healthcare services since its establishment in 2002. Equipped with state-of-the-art medical facilities, the hospital serves as a center for medical education, research, and clinical training.

Al Andalus Park:

Facts: Al Andalus Park is a testament to the city's commitment to providing accessible green spaces for its residents. The park features beautifully landscaped gardens, serene fountains, inviting walking paths, and engaging play areas. It has become a favored destination for families, fitness enthusiasts, and those seeking solace in the embrace of nature.

Madaba

Madaba, a city in central Jordan, is often referred to as the "City of Mosaics" due to its rich mosaic heritage. It's perhaps best known for the famous Madaba Map, an ancient mosaic depicting a map of the Holy Land. This historical treasure is housed in the St. George's Greek Orthodox Church.

The city's mosaic-making tradition continues to thrive, with artisans creating intricate pieces that are sought after by collectors and visitors alike. The Madaba Archaeological Park showcases a wealth of mosaics from different periods, offering a fascinating glimpse into the city's artistic legacy.

Madaba's historical significance extends beyond its mosaics. The city has roots dating back thousands of years, with archaeological sites like Tell Madaba revealing evidence of ancient settlements. The Madaba Archaeological Museum provides further insight into the region's history.

Aside from its cultural attractions, Madaba offers a charming atmosphere with its narrow, winding streets and bustling markets. Visitors can explore local handicraft shops, sample traditional Jordanian cuisine, and experience the warm hospitality of the residents.

Madaba's location on the King's Highway also makes it a convenient starting point for exploring other notable Jordanian sites, including Mount Nebo, where it's believed Moses saw the Promised Land, and the therapeutic waters of the Dead Sea.

Saint George's Greek Orthodox Church:

History: Saint George's Greek Orthodox Church in Madaba was constructed in the late 19th century on the site of an earlier church. The earlier church was dedicated to Saint George and was built around the 6th century.

Facts: The most renowned feature of this church is the mosaic map of the Holy Land, which is believed to date back to the 6th century. This remarkable mosaic is considered one of the oldest surviving maps of the Holy Land. It provides a fascinating glimpse into the geography, topography, and important biblical sites of the region during the Byzantine period. The map showcases cities, rivers, and even some architectural details with astonishing precision.

Madaba Archaeological Park:

History: The Madaba Archaeological Park is an expansive area that encompasses numerous archaeological sites in Madaba. It holds the remains of structures dating back to both the Byzantine and Umayyad periods.

Facts: Visitors to the park have the opportunity to explore the fascinating remnants of ancient Madaba. This includes the foundations of churches, houses, and other structures that once formed the heart of the city. The park provides valuable insights into the layout and architecture of Madaba during its rich historical past.

Madaba Mosaic School:

History: The Madaba Mosaic School was established to preserve and promote the ancient art of mosaic-making, a craft that has been deeply embedded in Madaba's cultural heritage for centuries.

Facts: The school offers workshops and courses dedicated to mosaic art, providing visitors with a unique opportunity to learn about the techniques and processes involved in creating intricate mosaic pieces. Participants can try their hand at this ancient craft under the guidance of skilled instructors, gaining an appreciation for the level of skill and artistry required to produce these stunning works.

Mount Nebo:

History: Mount Nebo holds immense biblical significance, as it is traditionally believed to be the place where Moses beheld the Promised Land before his passing.

Facts: From Mount Nebo's elevated vantage point, visitors are treated to breathtaking panoramic views. On clear days, the vista encompasses the Jordan Valley, the shimmering waters of the Dead Sea, and even parts of Jerusalem. The site is also home to the modern Memorial Church of Moses, which houses yet more magnificent mosaics. These artworks, along with the site's religious significance, draw pilgrims and tourists alike to this sacred location.

Madaba Archaeological Museum:

History: The Madaba Archaeological Museum was established to showcase the diverse array of archaeological finds from Madaba and the surrounding region.

Facts: Within its walls, the museum houses an extensive collection of artifacts that offer a comprehensive view of the area's history and culture. Visitors can marvel at items such as pottery, jewelry, and coins, each providing a unique window into the lives and customs of ancient inhabitants.

Haret Jdoudna:

History: Haret Jdoudna is a historic building that has undergone a transformation into a cultural center and restaurant, marrying the past with the present.

Facts: The establishment provides a captivating ambiance for visitors to savor traditional Jordanian cuisine. Guests can immerse themselves in an atmosphere that exudes warmth and hospitality. The combination of delicious food and a culturally-rich setting makes Haret Jdoudna a must-visit destination for those seeking an authentic Jordanian experience.

The Apostles Church:

History: The Apostles Church, dating back to the 6th century, stands as a testament to the enduring architectural and artistic legacy of Madaba.

Facts: Inside the church, visitors can marvel at the intricate mosaic decorations. These mosaics portray a range of scenes, including pastoral and hunting motifs. The level of detail and craftsmanship displayed in these artworks is a testament to the skill of the artisans of that era.

Madaba Archaeological Park Visitor Center:

History: The Madaba Archaeological Park Visitor Center was established to serve as an informative hub for visitors exploring the archaeological sites in the area.

Facts: The center offers a wealth of detailed information about the history, significance, and layout of the archaeological sites. It provides maps, guides, and expert advice to enhance the visitor's experience, ensuring that they gain a deeper appreciation for the cultural and historical heritage of Madaba.

Church of the Beheading of Saint John the Baptist:

History: This church is a place of reverence dedicated to Saint John the Baptist, believed to be the location where his head was laid to rest.

Facts: The church features a crypt that houses an altar and a revered icon of Saint John the Baptist. This site holds great religious significance for

Christians and serves as a place of pilgrimage and reflection.

Madaba Institute for Mosaic Art and Restoration (MIMAR):

History: MIMAR was established with the primary mission of training individuals in the art of mosaic-making and restoration, ensuring the preservation of this ancient craft.

Facts: The institute plays a pivotal role in safeguarding the legacy of mosaic art in Jordan. Through its programs, it equips individuals with the skills needed to create and restore intricate mosaic pieces. The efforts of MIMAR contribute significantly to the conservation and protection of historical mosaics in Jordan, ensuring that these cultural treasures continue to be appreciated for generations to come.

Madaba Archaeological Park West:

History: This section of the Madaba Archaeological Park is a treasure trove of Byzantine-era remains. It holds the remnants of houses that were inhabited during the Byzantine period. These houses contain fascinating architectural elements, including courtyards, cisterns, and living spaces.

Facts: Visitors who explore this area are treated to a well-preserved snapshot of daily life in Madaba during the Byzantine period. The architectural features provide valuable insights into how inhabitants of that era constructed and organized their living spaces. Walking among these ancient ruins, one can imagine the hustle and bustle of daily life that once filled these courtyards and rooms.

Madaba City Center:

History: Madaba City Center serves as the modern heartbeat of Madaba. It is a bustling hub of activity, with a rich tapestry of shops, restaurants, and local businesses.

Facts: The area is a vibrant and dynamic fusion of local markets, eateries, and commerce, offering visitors an authentic taste of contemporary Jordanian life. Strolling through the streets of Madaba City Center, one can witness the energetic rhythm of daily activities. Whether it's perusing local shops or savoring traditional cuisine, this district offers a unique opportunity to immerse oneself in the vibrant culture of the city.

Church of Apostles Mosaic Workshop:

History: This workshop stands as a testament to the dedication to preserving and continuing the ancient art of mosaic-making, a craft that has held a significant place in Madaba's cultural heritage for centuries.

Facts: Within the workshop, skilled artisans practice their craft, creating intricate mosaic pieces using traditional techniques passed down through generations. Visitors have the opportunity to witness the painstaking process of selecting and placing each individual tile to create stunning and detailed works of art. Moreover, the workshop offers mosaic art for sale, allowing visitors to take home a piece of this ancient tradition.

The Madaba Visitors Center:

History: The Madaba Visitors Center was established with the primary goal of enhancing the visitor experience in Madaba by providing valuable information about the city and its attractions.

Facts: The center is a valuable resource for visitors, offering a wealth of information about the history, culture, and points of interest in Madaba. It equips visitors with maps, guides, and other resources to help them navigate and make the most of their time in the city. The knowledgeable staff are on hand to offer advice and insights to ensure a fulfilling and enriching visit.

Madaba Art Gallery:

History: The Madaba Art Gallery stands as a vibrant showcase of contemporary Jordanian art, providing a platform for local artists to exhibit their creative works.

Facts: Visitors to the gallery are treated to a diverse array of art pieces, including paintings, sculptures, and other forms of visual art. Each piece offers a window into the artistic expression and cultural resonance of modern Jordan. The gallery serves as a testament to the thriving and dynamic art scene in Madaba, providing a space for both local and international artists to share their creativity.

The Madaba Mosque (Al-Hammam Mosque):

History: This mosque holds a prominent place in the religious landscape of Madaba.

Facts: The architectural design of the Al-Hammam Mosque reflects traditional Islamic styles, showcasing the elegant and timeless features characteristic of Islamic architecture. The mosque remains an integral center of worship and community gatherings for the local Muslim population, providing a space for spiritual reflection and communal connection.

Madaba Culture Palace:

History: The Madaba Culture Palace serves as a vital venue for cultural events and performances in Madaba.

Facts: The palace hosts a wide range of cultural activities, including music concerts, theatrical performances, exhibitions, and workshops. These events contribute to the cultural richness and vibrancy of the city, offering opportunities for both locals and visitors to engage with and appreciate various forms of artistic expression.

Madaba Archaeological Museum (South):

History: This section of the Madaba Archaeological Museum is dedicated to housing artifacts and displays that shed light on the history of the region.

Facts: Visitors to this museum section can explore an extensive collection of archaeological finds, including pottery, tools, and sculptures. These artifacts offer a fascinating glimpse into the ancient civilizations that once thrived in the Madaba region. Each item provides a piece of the puzzle in understanding the cultural and historical tapestry of the area.

Madaba Mosque (Al-Faqeer Mosque):

History: The Al-Faqeer Mosque stands as another significant place of worship in Madaba.

Facts: The mosque's architectural design pays homage to traditional Islamic styles, exemplifying the elegant and enduring features that define Islamic architecture. The mosque plays a pivotal role in the religious life of the local Muslim community, serving as a sanctuary for prayer, reflection, and communal gatherings.

Madaba Visitor Information Center:

History: The Madaba Visitor Information Center was established as a valuable resource for travelers seeking comprehensive information about Madaba and its attractions.

Facts: The center is staffed by knowledgeable personnel who are dedicated to assisting visitors in planning their exploration of Madaba. It provides an array of resources, including maps, brochures, and expert advice. The goal is to ensure that visitors have all the information they need to make the most of their time in the city, ensuring a fulfilling and enriching experience.

Petra

Petra, often hailed as the "Rose City," is an archaeological marvel nestled in the southern desert of Jordan. This UNESCO World Heritage site is renowned for its stunning rock-cut architecture, with intricate temples, tombs, and dwellings carved into vibrant red sandstone cliffs.

The city was the capital of the Nabatean Kingdom, and its history dates back to around 300 BCE. The most iconic structure is the Al-Khazneh, or "The Treasury," a magnificent mausoleum with a towering facade that captivates visitors as they emerge from the narrow Siq, a natural rock gorge.

Petra's archaeological expanse is vast, with countless archaeological sites, including the Monastery, the Royal Tombs, and the Great Temple, all revealing the advanced engineering and artistic prowess of the ancient Nabateans.

Beyond the archaeological wonders, Petra's landscape is awe-inspiring. The desert surroundings, with their unique geological formations, create a surreal backdrop for exploration. Trails lead to high vantage points offering panoramic views of the city and the surrounding valleys.

The intricate water management system of Petra, featuring channels, cisterns, and dams, showcases the ingenious engineering skills of its ancient inhabitants. This network allowed the city to flourish in an arid environment.

The Siq:

History: The Siq is a narrow gorge that serves as the main entrance to Petra. It was formed by tectonic forces and the erosion of water over millions of years.

Facts: As you walk through the Siq, you'll be flanked by towering cliffs that rise up to 200 meters. This natural pathway creates a dramatic and awe-inspiring entrance to the ancient city of Petra.

The Treasury (Al-Khazneh):

History: The Treasury is one of Petra's most iconic structures, believed to have been carved in the 1st century BC. It was initially a mausoleum and later used as a temple.

Facts: The facade of the Treasury is intricately decorated with classical Hellenistic architectural elements, and it's famously known for its intricate carvings and rose-red color, which glows beautifully in the morning sun.

The Street of Facades:

History: The Street of Facades is a row of monumental tombs carved into the cliffs. They were used as burial chambers for the Nabateans.

Facts: These facades are impressive in both their scale and detail. Some of the tombs have intricate decorations and inscriptions, showcasing the artistic skills of the Nabateans.

The Theater:

History: Carved into the mountainside, the Petra Theater dates back to the 1st century AD. It could accommodate up to 8,500 spectators.

Facts: The theater was used for various events, including theatrical performances and public gatherings. Its design is an example of the advanced engineering and architectural expertise of the Nabateans.

The Royal Tombs (including the Urn Tomb, Silk Tomb, Corinthian Tomb, and Palace Tomb):

History: These tombs were built for high-ranking officials and members of the Nabatean royal family. They were carved into the cliffs during the 1st century AD.

Facts: Each of these tombs is unique in its architectural style and decoration. The Urn Tomb, for example, is so named due to the large urn sculpture at its entrance.

The Monastery (Ad Deir):

History: The Monastery is one of Petra's largest and most impressive structures. It was built in the 1st century AD as a Nabatean tomb.

Facts: To reach the Monastery, visitors must climb over 800 steps. The facade of the Monastery is even larger than that of the Treasury, standing at approximately 47 meters in width and 48 meters in height.

The High Place of Sacrifice:

History: This site was used for religious ceremonies and offerings, possibly during the Nabatean period.

Facts: The High Place of Sacrifice offers a panoramic view of Petra, making it a significant and spiritually charged location. It's a testament to the Nabateans' reverence for the natural landscape.

The Great Temple:

History: The Great Temple complex was constructed during the 1st century BC and was a significant religious and ceremonial center in Petra.

Facts: The complex includes a large courtyard, a monumental staircase, and various chambers. The scale of the temple complex highlights the power and influence of the Nabateans.

The Garden Temple Complex:

History: This complex consists of several structures, including the Garden Temple, which was dedicated to the Nabatean god Dushara.

Facts: The Garden Temple was surrounded by lush gardens, showcasing the Nabateans' ability to cultivate vegetation in the desert environment.

The Petra Archaeological Museum:

History: The museum was established to showcase artifacts found in and around Petra.

Facts: It houses a collection of pottery, jewelry, tools, and other objects that provide insight into daily life in Petra during ancient times. The museum serves as an excellent complement to exploring the archaeological site.

The Colonnaded Street:

History: The Colonnaded Street is a partially-preserved ancient thoroughfare in Petra that was lined with columns and lined with shops.

Facts: This street was a bustling commercial hub, reflecting the prosperous trade and economic activity of Petra during its heyday. It's an excellent example of urban planning in the Nabatean city.

The Crusader Fort:

History: The Crusader Fort, also known as "Qal'at Al-Burj," was built by the Crusaders in the 12th century AD.

Facts: Although not originally built by the Nabateans, the fortification provides a unique perspective on the later history of Petra. It's strategically located to oversee the surrounding area.

The Lion Monument:

History: The Lion Monument is a rock relief carved into the sandstone cliffs of Petra, depicting a lion.

Facts: The significance and purpose of this carving remain uncertain. Some theories suggest it may have served as a boundary marker, while others propose it had a religious or symbolic meaning.

The Obelisk Tomb:

History: The Obelisk Tomb is one of the well-preserved tombs in Petra, known for its tall, slender shape.

Facts: The tomb gets its name from the four obelisks that crown its facade. The purpose of these obelisks is not entirely clear, but they are believed to have held some symbolic or religious significance for the Nabateans.

The Garden Triclinium:

History: The Garden Triclinium is a unique structure in Petra that was used for banquets or funerary feasts.

Facts: It features a central courtyard surrounded by chambers and a decorated facade. The location's name suggests that it may have been used for gatherings amidst a garden setting.

The Renaissance Tomb:

History: The Renaissance Tomb is a grand tomb in Petra, believed to have been built in the 1st century AD.

Facts: It's named "Renaissance Tomb" due to its intricate facade and grandeur. The tomb's design reflects a level of architectural sophistication and artistic prowess characteristic of the Nabateans.

The Sextius Florentinus Tomb:

History: This tomb is named after its Latin inscription, which mentions a Roman governor of Arabia named Sextius Florentinus.

Facts: The tomb provides valuable historical insight into the interaction between the Nabateans and the Roman Empire. It stands as a testament to the political and cultural dynamics of the region during antiquity.

The Triclinium:

History: The Triclinium is a funerary banquet hall, reflecting the Nabatean tradition of hosting feasts in honor of the deceased.

Facts: The hall is adorned with ornate carvings and decorations, highlighting the importance of ritual and commemoration in Nabatean culture. It's a testament to the rich and multifaceted cultural practices of the ancient city.

The Tomb of Uneishu:

History: The Tomb of Uneishu is a well-preserved tomb in Petra, believed to be from the 2nd century AD.

Facts: The tomb is named after the person it was built for, Uneishu, who was likely a wealthy and prominent individual in Nabatean society. Its architectural elegance and detailed carvings reflect the status and significance of its occupant.

The Roman Soldier Tomb:

History: The Roman Soldier Tomb is named due to the carving of a Roman soldier on its facade.

Facts: The presence of a Roman soldier figure suggests some level of Roman influence or interaction in Petra. This tomb is an example of how different cultures and styles intersected in the ancient city.

Salt

. Salt, chemically known as sodium chloride ($NaCl$), is a fundamental compound essential for various biological and industrial processes. It is composed of sodium ions and chloride ions, which are vital for maintaining fluid balance in living organisms, transmitting nerve impulses, and aiding in muscle function. Additionally, salt is a natural flavor enhancer and preservative in food, playing a crucial role in culinary applications.

In industrial settings, salt finds widespread use in areas such as chemical production, water treatment, and metallurgy. It is a key component in processes like the manufacture of chlorine and caustic soda, as well as in the production of glass, detergents, and textiles. Moreover, salt is employed for de-icing roads in colder climates, preventing the formation of ice on roadways during winter months.

Beyond its practical applications, salt has cultural and historical significance. It has been valued for centuries as a trade commodity and has influenced societies in terms of economic development and geopolitics. In some cultures, salt holds symbolic importance and is used in rituals and ceremonies.

However, excessive salt consumption can lead to health issues, including high blood pressure and cardiovascular diseases. Therefore, it is crucial to strike a balance between the benefits and potential risks associated with salt intake.

Al-Hammam Street:

Our journey begins on Al-Hammam Street, the vibrant heart of Salt's historic district. This bustling market street is lined with colorful shops, selling everything from spices and textiles to handmade crafts.

Abu Jaber House:

A short walk from Al-Hammam Street brings us to the Abu Jaber House, a beautifully restored Ottoman-era mansion. It offers a glimpse into the architectural grandeur of the past, with its intricate woodwork and traditional Jordanian design.

Great Mosque:

Just a stone's throw away stands the Great Mosque, a magnificent example of Islamic architecture. It dates back to the 14th century and features a stunning courtyard and an intricately decorated prayer hall.

Archaeological and Folklore Museum:

Let's continue our journey to the Archaeological and Folklore Museum. Here, you can explore a fascinating collection of artifacts that offer insights into the history and culture of Salt and its surroundings.

As-Salt Archaeological Park:

Our next stop is the As-Salt Archaeological Park, where you can wander among the ancient ruins that bear witness to the city's rich history. From Roman to Ottoman remains, this site offers a captivating journey through time.

Al-Khader Church:

Moving on, we visit Al-Khader Church, a significant religious site for both Christians and Muslims. The church's architecture is a blend of Romanesque and Byzantine styles, and it houses beautiful frescoes.

The Ottoman Railway Station:

Next, we head to the Ottoman Railway Station, an iconic landmark that played a crucial role in Jordan's transportation history. The station has been meticulously restored and now serves as a cultural center.

The Royal Film Commission:

For a touch of modern cultural immersion, let's visit the Royal Film Commission, where you can learn about Jordan's burgeoning film industry and catch a screening of a locally produced film.

Rainbow Street:

we'll head to Rainbow Street, a trendy boulevard known for its vibrant atmosphere, cafes, and boutique shops. It's a perfect place to relax, enjoy a cup of coffee, and soak in the local ambiance.

Al-Mazar Al-Shamali:

Let's venture a bit further to Al-Mazar Al-Shamali, a picturesque area located to the north of Salt. Here, you'll find serene landscapes, olive groves, and charming villages, providing a peaceful contrast to the bustling city center.

Al-Salt Amman Street Market:

If you're interested in experiencing local life, a visit to Al-Salt Amman Street Market is a must. This lively market is known for its fresh produce, spices, and a wide variety of goods. It's a great place to interact with locals and get a taste of everyday Jordanian life.

Al-Bayader Wadi:

For nature enthusiasts, a visit to Al-Bayader Wadi is a wonderful opportunity to explore Jordan's scenic countryside. This wadi (valley) offers hiking trails, waterfalls, and a chance to immerse yourself in the natural beauty of the region.

Al-Ain Plaza:

If you're in the mood for some shopping, Al-Ain Plaza is a modern shopping complex where you can find a range of stores selling clothing, electronics, and local handicrafts.

Al-Salt City Mall:

For a more comprehensive shopping experience, Al-Salt City Mall offers a wide array of shops, restaurants, and entertainment options. It's a great place to unwind and indulge in some retail therapy.

Umm Qais:

While not in Salt itself, Umm Qais is a nearby archaeological site that is well worth a visit. It offers stunning panoramic views of the Sea of Galilee, the Golan Heights, and the Yarmouk River, along with impressive Roman ruins.

WHERE TO EAT

Amman:

Wild Jordan Center (Downtown Amman):

Nestled in the heart of Amman, this eco-friendly restaurant offers a delightful mix of traditional Jordanian cuisine with a modern twist. The panoramic views of the city from the terrace are a bonus!

Hashem Restaurant (Downtown Amman):

A true culinary institution in Amman, Hashem's has been serving mouthwatering Jordanian street food for generations. Their falafel and hummus are legendary!

Sufra Restaurant (Rainbow Street):

Sufra, with its warm and inviting atmosphere, offers a taste of authentic Jordanian home cooking. From mansaf to maqluba, every dish here is a delightful journey through Jordan's culinary heritage.

Aqaba:

Ali Baba Restaurant (Aqaba City Center):

Located along Aqaba's picturesque waterfront, Ali Baba serves up a delectable selection of seafood dishes. The catch of the day is always a highlight!

Boulevard Café (Tala Bay):

For a more upscale dining experience, Boulevard Café in Tala Bay offers a fusion of international and local flavors. The sea views from the terrace make it a perfect spot for a romantic dinner.

Irbid:

Café De La Paix (Downtown Irbid):

This charming café is a favorite among locals and visitors alike. Whether you're in the mood for a hearty breakfast or a leisurely afternoon coffee, Café De La Paix is a welcoming retreat.

Bawabit Al Sham (Al Hasan Industrial City):

For a taste of traditional Jordanian comfort food, Bawabit Al Sham is the place to go. Their hearty stews and grilled meats are sure to satisfy your appetite.

Madaba:

Haret Jdoudna (Madaba City Center):

Set in a beautifully restored traditional house, Haret Jdoudna offers a diverse menu that showcases Jordanian and Middle Eastern cuisine. The serene courtyard is a perfect spot to savor your meal.

Queen Ayola (Madaba City Center):

Known for its friendly staff and delightful desserts, Queen Ayola is a popular spot for those with a sweet tooth. Be sure to try their knafeh, a delectable Jordanian pastry.

Petra:

My Mom's Recipe (Wadi Musa):

This family-run restaurant serves up delicious Jordanian comfort food that feels like a home-cooked meal. The warm hospitality and flavorful dishes make it a must-visit in Petra.

Al Qantarah Restaurant (Wadi Musa):

Offering a mix of local and international cuisine, Al Qantarah is a great place to refuel after exploring the ancient city of Petra. The terrace provides stunning views of the surrounding mountains.

Salt:

Beit Aziz (Downtown Salt):

Housed in a beautifully restored historic building, Beit Aziz offers a range of Jordanian dishes made with locally sourced ingredients. The ambiance here is both elegant and inviting.

Zuwar Restaurant (Downtown Salt):

With its cozy atmosphere and flavorful dishes, Zuwar is a popular choice for those looking to experience the taste of authentic Jordanian cuisine in Salt. Their lamb dishes are particularly recommended.

Direction how to get there

Amman:

Wild Jordan Center (Downtown Amman):

Address: Othman Ben Affan Street, Jabal Amman, Amman

Directions: From Downtown, head west on King Faisal Street. Turn left onto Othman Ben Affan Street. The restaurant will be on your right.

Hashem Restaurant (Downtown Amman):

Address: Al-Amir Mohammed St., Downtown, Amman

Directions: Located near the Roman Theater, Hashem Restaurant is a well-known landmark in Downtown Amman.

Sufra Restaurant (Rainbow Street):

Address: 17 Rainbow St., Amman

Directions: Head west on Rainbow Street from First Circle. The restaurant will be on your right.

Aqaba:

Ali Baba Restaurant (Aqaba City Center):

Address: Al-Sakani St., Aqaba

Directions: Located along the Aqaba waterfront, Ali Baba Restaurant is easily accessible from the city center.

Boulevard Café (Tala Bay):

Address: Tala Bay, Aqaba

Directions: Follow the main road to Tala Bay. The café is located within the Tala Bay Resort complex.

Irbid:

Café De La Paix (Downtown Irbid):

Address: Al-Yarmouk St., Irbid

Directions: Located in the heart of Downtown Irbid, easily accessible from the main streets.

Bawabit Al Sham (Al Hasan Industrial City):

Address: Al Hasan Industrial City, Irbid

Directions: Follow signs to Al Hasan Industrial City. The restaurant is located within the industrial area.

Madaba:

Haret Jdoudna (Madaba City Center):

Address: 23 Al-Yarmouk St., Madaba

Directions: Located in the city center of Madaba, near the St. George's Church.

Address: 5 Al-Mahdi St., Madaba

Directions: Easily accessible from the main streets of Madaba city center.

Petra:

My Mom's Recipe (Wadi Musa):

Address: Tourism St., Wadi Musa

Directions: Located on the main road leading to Petra's archaeological site.

Al Qantarah Restaurant (Wadi Musa):

Address: Tourism St., Wadi Musa

Directions: Situated on the main road of Wadi Musa, near the entrance to Petra.

Salt:

Beit Aziz (Downtown Salt):

Address: Omar Al-Maani St., Downtown Salt

Directions: Located in the historic downtown area of Salt, near Al-Hammam Street.

Zuwar Restaurant (Downtown Salt):

Address: Al-Hammam St., Downtown Salt

Directions: Easily accessible from Al-Hammam Street, in the heart of Downtown Salt.

TOP ATTRACTIONS IN JORDAN

Petra:

History: Petra is undoubtedly Jordan's most famous attraction. This ancient city, carved into rose-red cliffs by the Nabateans over 2,000 years ago, served as a thriving trade hub and capital of the Nabatean Kingdom. It was a crucial junction for the silk and spice trade routes that connected Arabia, Egypt, and the Mediterranean.

Facts:

Petra's most iconic structure is the Treasury (Al-Khazneh), a monumental tomb with intricate Hellenistic and Eastern architectural elements.

The city's archaeological wealth is immense, featuring thousands of tombs, temples, and dwellings.

Petra was "rediscovered" by a Swiss explorer named Johann Ludwig Burckhardt in 1812, although it was known to local Bedouins.

Wadi Rum:

History: Wadi Rum, often called the "Valley of the Moon," has been inhabited by various cultures over millennia, including the Nabateans and the Bedouin tribes. It's known for its stunning desert landscapes and unique rock formations.

Facts:

Lawrence of Arabia made Wadi Rum famous during World War I, using it as a base of operations.

Many scenes from the movie "Lawrence of Arabia" were filmed in Wadi Rum.

Dead Sea:

History: The Dead Sea, one of the saltiest bodies of water in the world, has been a historical and natural wonder for thousands of years. It's believed to be the site of biblical cities like Sodom and Gomorrah.

Facts:

The high salt concentration makes it nearly impossible for plants and animals to thrive, hence the name "Dead Sea."

The therapeutic properties of the Dead Sea mud and minerals have attracted visitors for centuries.

Jerash:

History: Jerash is one of the best-preserved Roman cities in the world. It was originally settled by Alexander the Great and later became a prominent Roman city in the Decapolis League.

Facts:

Notable structures include the Temple of Artemis, the Oval Plaza, and the well-preserved Hadrian's Arch.

The city's ancient Roman ruins offer a vivid glimpse into daily life during the Roman period.

Amman Citadel:

History: The Amman Citadel, situated on a hill in downtown Amman, has been inhabited for thousands of years. It has seen the rise and fall of many civilizations, including the Romans and the Umayyads.

Facts:

The Citadel features the Temple of Hercules, the Umayyad Palace, and the Byzantine Church.

The site offers panoramic views of Amman, showcasing the city's modern and ancient juxtaposition.

Aqaba and the Red Sea:

History: Aqaba is Jordan's only coastal city, and its strategic location has made it a historically significant port for trade routes in the region.

Facts:

The Red Sea is renowned for its vibrant coral reefs, making Aqaba a popular destination for diving and snorkeling enthusiasts.

The city is mentioned in historical texts dating back to the 4th century BCE.

Mount Nebo:

History: Mount Nebo is a significant biblical site mentioned in the Old Testament. According to tradition, it is where Moses saw the Promised Land before his passing.

Facts:

The site offers breathtaking views of the Jordan Valley, the Dead Sea, and even Jerusalem on a clear day.

The Memorial Church of Moses on Mount Nebo houses ancient mosaics that date back to the 4th century.

Madaba and the Mosaic Map:

History: Madaba is known as the "City of Mosaics" due to its rich tradition of mosaic art. The highlight is the Mosaic Map, an ancient floor mosaic that depicts the Holy Land and Jerusalem during the Byzantine period.

Facts:

The Mosaic Map is considered one of the oldest known maps of the Holy Land.

Madaba is mentioned in historical texts dating back to the 9th century BCE.

Kerak Castle:

History: Kerak Castle, also known as Al-Karak, is a massive Crusader fortress constructed in the 12th century. It played a crucial role in the Crusades and witnessed numerous battles.

Facts:

The castle is an impressive example of Crusader military architecture, featuring thick walls, tunnels, and strategic defensive positions.

It was the stronghold of the notorious Reynald of Chatillon, a key figure in Crusader history.

Qasr Amra:

History: Qasr Amra is a desert castle that dates back to the early Islamic period, built by the Umayyad Caliphate. It served as a leisure retreat for caliphs and is known for its exquisite frescoes.

Facts:

The frescoes in Qasr Amra depict a wide range of subjects, including hunting scenes, musicians, and zodiac symbols, providing a unique glimpse into Umayyad art and culture.

It is a UNESCO World Heritage site and is often referred to as the "Desert Castle of Jordan."

Umm Qais:

History: Umm Qais, also known as Gadara in ancient times, was a Greco-Roman city and a member of the Decapolis. It was a thriving cultural and economic center.

Facts:

The site offers stunning panoramic views of the Sea of Galilee, the Golan Heights, and the Yarmouk River, providing a testament to its strategic importance in antiquity.

Umm Qais is mentioned in historical texts dating back to the 3rd century BCE.

Ajloun Castle:

History: Ajloun Castle, also known as Qal'at Ar-Rabad, was constructed in the 12th century by Salah ad-Din (Saladin) to defend against Crusader attacks.

Facts:

The castle is a prime example of Islamic military architecture, featuring strategic towers and defensive walls.

Ajloun Castle offers panoramic views of the surrounding forests and countryside.

Direction how to get there

Petra:

From Amman, take the Desert Highway south. Follow signs for Petra. The archaeological site is well-marked and easily accessible.

Wadi Rum:

Wadi Rum is located about 60 kilometers south of Petra. It's best to arrange transportation through a tour operator or hire a local guide.

Dead Sea:

From Amman, take the Dead Sea Highway west. Follow signs to the Dead Sea resorts and beaches.

Jerash:

From Amman, head north on Jerash-Amman Road. Follow signs to the ancient city of Jerash.

Amman Citadel:

The Citadel is located in the heart of Amman. It's easily accessible by car or on foot from downtown Amman.

Aqaba and the Red Sea:

Aqaba is easily reached by car or bus from other parts of Jordan. If you're coming from Amman, it's about a 4-hour drive south on the Desert Highway.

Mount Nebo:

From Amman, take the Dead Sea Highway south. Follow signs to Mount Nebo. It's approximately a 40-minute drive.

Madaba and the Mosaic Map:

Madaba is located southwest of Amman. Follow signs to Madaba from Amman. The Mosaic Map is located in St. George's Church in the city center.

Kerak Castle:

Kerak is about a 2-hour drive south of Amman. Follow signs to Kerak from the Desert Highway.

Qasr Amra:

Qasr Amra is located in the eastern desert of Jordan. It's best to arrange transportation through a tour operator or hire a local guide.

Umm Qais:

Umm Qais is located in the far north of Jordan. It's about a 2.5-hour drive from Amman. Follow signs to Umm Qais.

Ajloun Castle:

Ajloun is about a 1.5-hour drive north of Amman. Follow signs to Ajloun Castle from the main road.

TOP OUTDOOR ACTIVITIES IN JORDAN

Hiking and Trekking:

Jordan boasts a network of scenic trails that wind through its deserts, mountains, and nature reserves. The most famous trek is the Jordan Trail, a 650-kilometer trail that spans the length of the country, offering a diverse range of terrains and breathtaking vistas.

Desert Safaris:

Explore the mesmerizing landscapes of Wadi Rum and other desert regions via a guided jeep safari. Traverse sand dunes, explore ancient petroglyphs, and witness stunning rock formations as you navigate the vast desert terrain.

Canyoning and Rock Climbing:

Wadi Mujib, Jordan's "Grand Canyon," offers thrilling canyoning adventures, where you'll navigate through narrow gorges, rappel down waterfalls, and swim through refreshing pools. For rock climbing enthusiasts, Wadi Rum provides world-class opportunities to scale its unique sandstone cliffs.

Diving and Snorkeling:

Aqaba, located on the Red Sea coast, is a diver's paradise. Its clear waters teem with vibrant marine life and colorful coral reefs. Whether you're a certified diver or a beginner looking to try snorkeling, the Red Sea offers unforgettable underwater experiences.

Hot Air Ballooning:

Soar above the landscapes of Wadi Rum in a hot air balloon for a bird's-eye view of the desert's iconic rock formations, vast sand dunes, and serene valleys. This offers a unique perspective on the stunning desert scenery.

Camping Under the Stars:

Spending a night in the desert is a must-do experience in Jordan. Whether in Wadi Rum, the Dana Biosphere Reserve, or other remote locations, camping allows you to fully immerse yourself in the tranquility and beauty of Jordan's natural surroundings.

Biking and Cycling:

Explore Jordan's diverse landscapes on two wheels. From the rugged trails of Wadi Rum to the scenic routes along the Dead Sea, biking offers an exhilarating way to experience the country's varied terrain.

Birdwatching and Wildlife Viewing:

Jordan is home to several bird sanctuaries and nature reserves, such as Azraq Wetland Reserve and Dana Biosphere Reserve. These areas provide excellent opportunities to observe a wide variety of bird species and other wildlife in their natural habitats.

Balloon Rides Over Luxor:

For a truly unique experience, consider taking a hot air balloon ride over the ancient city of Luxor. As you float above the Nile River and the Valley of the Kings, you'll witness the stunning sunrise illuminating the historic sites below.

Stargazing and Astronomy Tours:

Jordan's clear skies and minimal light pollution make it an ideal destination for stargazing. Joining an astronomy tour or simply lying under the open sky in a desert location like Wadi Rum can provide a mesmerizing view of the night sky.

Camel Trekking:

Embark on a traditional mode of transport and explore the desert landscapes in style. Riding a camel allows you to experience the slower pace of life in the desert, giving you a unique connection with the environment.

Kayaking and Rafting:

The crystal-clear waters of the Mujib and Zarqa Ma'in rivers offer exciting opportunities for kayaking and white-water rafting. Navigate through canyons, waterfalls, and scenic gorges for an exhilarating aquatic adventure.

Paragliding:

Experience the thrill of flight with a paragliding adventure in locations like Aqaba and Wadi Rum. Soar above the stunning landscapes, taking in panoramic views of Jordan's diverse terrain.

Yoga and Wellness Retreats:

Many resorts and retreat centers in Jordan offer yoga and wellness programs set against the backdrop of serene natural surroundings. Reconnect with your inner self while surrounded by the beauty of Jordan's landscapes.

Cultural Experiences with Bedouin Tribes:

Engage with Jordan's Bedouin communities for an authentic cultural experience. Join guided tours or stay in traditional Bedouin camps to learn about their customs, traditions, and way of life.

Archery and Shooting:

Some desert camps in places like Wadi Rum offer archery and shooting experiences. Test your aim and have fun with these unique activities against the stunning desert backdrop.

Exploring Nature Reserves:

Jordan is home to several nature reserves, including Dana Biosphere Reserve and Azraq Wetland Reserve. These protected areas offer opportunities for guided nature walks, wildlife spotting, and birdwatching.

EXPLORING JORDAN CUISINE

Jordan's strategic location at the crossroads of Asia, Africa, and Europe has not only made it a historical focal point but has also deeply influenced its culinary traditions. The country's diverse landscape plays a pivotal role in shaping the ingredients and flavors that define Jordanian cuisine.

The Fertile Jordan Valley, with its abundant water supply from the Jordan River, provides a fertile ground for growing a variety of fruits and vegetables. This region is known for its lush orchards producing olives, citrus fruits, and a plethora of fresh produce. These bountiful harvests contribute to the vibrant and colorful array of ingredients used in Jordanian dishes.

Conversely, the arid desert terrain of Wadi Rum, with its rugged sandstone formations and vast expanses of red sands, showcases the resourcefulness of the Bedouin communities. In this harsh environment, traditional techniques such as underground pit cooking (Zarb) have been developed, allowing for the preparation of succulent, slow-cooked meats using limited resources.

Key Ingredients:

Olive Oil:

Jordanian olive oil is often referred to as "liquid gold" for good reason. The country boasts some of the oldest olive groves in the world, with trees that have stood for centuries. The rich, fruity, and robust flavors of Jordanian olive oil are a hallmark of the cuisine, used generously in salads, dips, and as a cooking medium.

Grains:

Wheat, barley, and rice form the foundation of Jordanian cuisine. These versatile grains are transformed into an array of dishes, from the ubiquitous flatbreads to hearty pilafs and comforting soups.

Herbs and Spices:

Aromatic herbs and spices play a pivotal role in flavoring Jordanian dishes. Mint, parsley, cumin, coriander, and the distinctive tang of sumac are just a few examples. These ingredients add depth, fragrance, and character to everything from savory stews to refreshing salads.

Legumes:

Lentils, chickpeas, and fava beans are nutritional powerhouses and staples in Jordanian cooking. They are the building blocks of nourishing soups, hearty stews, and iconic dishes like falafel and hummus.

Meats:

While lamb is the centerpiece of many Jordanian meat dishes, the culinary landscape also embraces a variety of proteins including chicken, beef, and goat. The versatility of these meats is reflected in the diverse range of preparations, from slow-cooked delicacies to succulent grilled kebabs.

Signature Dishes:

Each signature Jordanian dish is a testament to the rich tapestry of flavors and techniques woven into the country's culinary heritage:

Mansaf:

Considered the crown jewel of Jordanian cuisine, Mansaf is a dish that embodies the essence of celebration and togetherness. The tender, slow-cooked lamb, bathed in a velvety yogurt sauce infused with dried yoghurt (jameed), is served atop a mound of fragrant rice. It's a symphony of flavors and textures, best enjoyed on special occasions and gatherings.

Maqluba:

This culinary masterpiece is a testament to Jordanian ingenuity. Layers of rice, vegetables, and meat are meticulously arranged, then cooked together to create a harmonious medley of flavors. When inverted onto a platter, Maqluba reveals its visually stunning presentation, making it as delightful to the eyes as it is to the palate.

Musakhan:

Comfort food at its finest, Musakhan showcases the ingenious use of sumac in Jordanian cuisine. Roasted chicken, fragrant with the tartness of sumac, is adorned with caramelized onions and served on a bed of warm flatbread. It's a dish that resonates with both simplicity and sophistication.

Zarb:

Rooted in the traditions of the Bedouin communities, Zarb exemplifies the resourcefulness born of desert living. Meats and vegetables are slow-cooked in an underground pit, resulting in succulent, smoky flavors that pay homage to the natural bounty of the land.

Knafeh:

The Jordanian dessert landscape finds its sweet crescendo in Knafeh. Layers of delicate pastry are soaked in luscious syrup, encasing a heart of either melted cheese or clotted cream. This delectable blend of sweet and savory flavors is a fitting finale to any Jordanian meal.

FESTIVAL AND EVENTS IN JORDAN

jerash Festival:

History: The Jerash Festival, held annually in the ancient city of Jerash, has deep historical roots dating back to the 1980s. It was initially established to revive and showcase Jordan's cultural heritage, and has since evolved into one of the most prominent cultural events in the region.

Beauty: Set against the awe-inspiring backdrop of Jerash's well-preserved Roman ruins, the festival transforms the archaeological site into a bustling hub of artistic expression. Visitors are treated to a diverse program of music, dance, theater, and exhibitions, creating a mesmerizing fusion of the ancient and the contemporary.

Al Balad Music Festival:

History: The Al Balad Music Festival, held in Amman's historic downtown district, Al Balad, is a celebration of Jordan's musical heritage. It was inaugurated in 1996 and has since become a cherished event for music enthusiasts and cultural aficionados.

Beauty: The festival takes place amidst the enchanting ambiance of Al Balad, where ancient stone buildings and narrow winding streets provide a captivating backdrop for performances. Musicians from Jordan and around the world come together to showcase a diverse range of musical genres, creating a symphony of sounds that reverberate through the heart of the city.

Petra By Night:

History: Although not a traditional festival, Petra By Night is a magical and evocative event that allows visitors to experience the ancient city of Petra in a unique and enchanting way. The tradition of Petra By Night has been ongoing for several decades.

Beauty: As night falls, the Siq, a narrow gorge leading to Petra's famed Treasury, is illuminated by thousands of candles, casting a warm, golden glow on the rose-red sandstone cliffs. Visitors are led through the candlelit pathway to reach the Treasury, where they are treated to a mesmerizing performance of Bedouin music, allowing them to connect with the ancient spirit of this UNESCO World Heritage site.

Jordan Rally:

History: The Jordan Rally, part of the FIA World Rally Championship, has been a prominent event on the international motorsport calendar since 2008. It is a testament to Jordan's commitment to hosting world-class sporting events.

Beauty: The rally takes place against the backdrop of Jordan's diverse landscapes, from the challenging desert terrains to the scenic mountain roads. Spectators have the opportunity to witness high-speed action amidst the stunning natural beauty of Jordan, making it a unique and thrilling experience for motorsport enthusiasts.

Eid al-Fitr and Eid al-Adha:

History: These two Islamic holidays hold deep religious and cultural significance in Jordan and are celebrated by Muslims worldwide. Eid al-Fitr marks the end of Ramadan, while Eid al-Adha commemorates the willingness of Ibrahim (Abraham) to sacrifice his son as an act of obedience to God.

Beauty: The festivities during these holidays are a testament to Jordanian hospitality and the strong sense of community. Families come together to share special meals, exchange gifts, and engage in acts of charity. The streets are adorned with colorful decorations, and people wear their finest traditional clothing, creating an atmosphere of joy and unity.

Ajloun International Film Festival:

History: Established in 2010, the Ajloun International Film Festival has become a significant cultural event in Jordan. It aims to promote the art of filmmaking and provide a platform for local and international filmmakers to showcase their work.

Beauty: Set against the backdrop of the picturesque Ajloun Castle and the lush greenery of the Ajloun Forest Reserve, the festival creates a unique blend of history, culture, and cinematic artistry. Attendees have the opportunity to watch a diverse selection of films, attend workshops, and engage with filmmakers, all while surrounded by the natural beauty of the Jordanian countryside.

Amman Jazz Festival:

History: The Amman Jazz Festival, inaugurated in 2012, celebrates the universal language of music by bringing together jazz musicians from Jordan and around the world. It has quickly become a highlight for music lovers in the region.

Beauty: The festival takes place in various venues across Amman, with performances held in parks, historic sites, and modern auditoriums. Against the backdrop of the city's diverse urban landscape, attendees are treated to an eclectic mix of jazz styles, creating an atmosphere of artistic expression and cultural exchange.

Jordan Fashion Week:

History: Launched in 2013, Jordan Fashion Week has become a significant platform for designers and fashion enthusiasts in the region. It showcases the talent and creativity of Jordan's burgeoning fashion industry.

Beauty: The event takes place in upscale venues in Amman, with runway shows featuring both established and emerging designers. Against the backdrop of contemporary fashion, attendees are treated to a fusion of innovative designs and traditional craftsmanship, reflecting Jordan's evolving cultural landscape.

Dead Sea Ultra Marathon:

History: The Dead Sea Ultra Marathon, established in 1993, is a testament to Jordan's commitment to promoting sports and adventure tourism. It has gained international recognition as one of the world's most unique and challenging ultra-marathons.

Beauty: The race course stretches along the shores of the Dead Sea, the lowest point on Earth. Runners are treated to breathtaking views of the sea's tranquil waters and the rugged landscapes of the surrounding mountains. The event not only provides a physical challenge but also allows participants to connect with the natural beauty and geological wonders of Jordan.

TOP ACCOMMODATION IN JORDAN

Amman:

Four Seasons Hotel Amman

Location: 5th Circle, Al-Kindi Street, Amman

Description: A luxurious 5-star hotel offering opulent rooms, exquisite dining options, a spa, and stunning views of the city. It's known for its impeccable service and top-notch amenities.

. Amman Rotana

Location: Abdali, Black Iris Street, Amman

Description: A modern and stylish 5-star hotel in the heart of Amman's new downtown, featuring elegant rooms, multiple dining options, a rooftop pool, and a wellness center.

Aqaba:

Kempinski Hotel Aqaba Red Sea

Location: King Hussein Street, Aqaba

Description: A luxurious beachfront resort offering lavish rooms, private beach access, a range of restaurants and bars, a spa, and breathtaking views of the Red Sea.

Movenpick Resort & Spa Tala Bay Aqaba

Location: South Beach Road, Aqaba

Description: Situated in the scenic Tala Bay area, this 5-star resort boasts well-appointed rooms, private beach access, multiple dining options, a spa, and a range of water activities.

Irbid:

Olive Branch Hotel

Location: Al-Hoson, Irbid

Description: A comfortable and welcoming hotel with well-appointed rooms, a restaurant serving local and international cuisine, and a friendly staff that ensures a pleasant stay.

Rum Art Hotel

Location: Al-Hoson, Irbid

Description: A boutique hotel featuring uniquely designed rooms, an art gallery, and a cozy atmosphere. It's a great choice for travelers seeking a more intimate accommodation experience.

Madaba:

Mosaic City Hotel

Location: King Talal Street, Madaba

Description: A charming hotel in the heart of Madaba, known for its friendly staff, comfortable rooms, and a rooftop terrace offering panoramic views of the city and its famous mosaics.

Mariam Hotel

Location: King Talal Street, Madaba

Description: A budget-friendly option with clean and comfortable rooms, located near the St. George's Church. The hotel provides a convenient base for exploring Madaba's attractions.

Petra:

Movenpick Resort Petra

Location: Wadi Musa, Petra

Description: Situated right at the entrance to Petra, this 5-star resort offers elegant rooms, stunning views of the mountains, multiple dining options, and a rooftop terrace with a pool.

Petra Guest House Hotel

Location: Wadi Musa, Petra

Description: A comfortable hotel with a prime location, just steps away from the entrance to Petra. It offers cozy rooms, a restaurant, and a terrace with views of the archaeological site.

Salt:

Mountain Breeze Resort

Location: Dibeen Forest Reserve, Salt

Description: Nestled in the serene Dibeen Forest, this eco-friendly resort offers cozy chalets, a restaurant serving organic cuisine, and opportunities for outdoor activities like hiking and birdwatching.

The Old Salt Road

Location: Downtown, Salt

Description: Housed in a beautifully restored historic building, this boutique hotel offers a blend of old-world charm and modern comfort. It features elegantly decorated rooms and a courtyard cafe.

SHOPPINMG IN JORDAN

Amman:

Rainbow Street:

Description: Located in the heart of Amman, Rainbow Street is a bustling thoroughfare known for its vibrant atmosphere and eclectic mix of shops. Here, you'll find boutique stores, art galleries, souvenir shops, and trendy cafes. It's an excellent place to pick up unique gifts, local crafts, and stylish clothing.

Al Balad - Downtown Amman:

Description: The historic downtown area of Amman is a treasure trove of shops and markets. You can explore the Souk Jara, a weekly market where local artisans and craftspeople sell their wares. Additionally, you'll find shops offering traditional Jordanian clothing, spices, textiles, and antiques.

The Boulevard:

Description: Situated in the modern Abdali district, The Boulevard is a contemporary shopping destination featuring a mix of high-end fashion boutiques, international brands, cafes, and restaurants. It's a great place for upscale shopping and leisurely strolls.

Al-Wakalat Street (The Sweifieh Shopping District):

Description: This bustling commercial district in Amman is home to numerous malls and shops, including Wakalat Street Mall. Here, you'll find a wide range of fashion outlets, both local and international, offering clothing, accessories, and footwear.

Aqaba:

Aqaba City Center Mall:

Description: As Aqaba's largest shopping mall, City Center offers a wide array of shops, ranging from fashion and beauty to electronics and home goods. It's a one-stop destination for both international and local brands.

Ayla Oasis Plaza:

Description: Located in the scenic Ayla development, this shopping plaza offers a mix of boutique stores, designer outlets, and dining options. Visitors can shop for fashion, jewelry, and unique gifts while enjoying views of the marina.

Souk by the Sea:

Description: For a more traditional shopping experience, Souk by the Sea is a lively market located along Aqaba's waterfront. It's a great place to find local handicrafts, spices, souvenirs, and traditional Jordanian clothing.

Irbid:

Arabela Mall:

Description: Arabela Mall is one of Irbid's prominent shopping destinations, offering a diverse range of stores, including clothing boutiques, electronics shops, and eateries. It's a popular spot for both locals and visitors.

Yarmouk Complex:

Description: Located in the heart of Irbid, the Yarmouk Complex is a bustling commercial center featuring various shops, from clothing and accessories to electronics and household items. It's a convenient place for shopping in the city.

Madaba:

Madaba Handicrafts Center:

Description: This center showcases the rich tradition of Jordanian craftsmanship. Visitors can find intricately designed mosaics, pottery, and other handcrafted items, all made by local artisans. It's an ideal place to pick up unique souvenirs.

Madaba Souk:

Description: The bustling souk in Madaba's city center offers a wide range of goods, including textiles, spices, ceramics, and jewelry. It's a great place to experience the local market culture and find authentic Jordanian products.

Petra:

Petra Craft Center:

Description: Situated near the entrance to Petra, this center features a selection of handcrafted items made by local artisans. Visitors can find beautifully carved stone pieces, jewelry, textiles, and souvenirs inspired by the region's history and culture.

Al-Siq Street:

Description: As the main street leading to the entrance of Petra, Al-Siq Street is lined with stalls and shops selling a variety of handicrafts, jewelry, and traditional Jordanian goods. It's a convenient place for shopping before or after exploring the archaeological site.

Salt:

Souq Al-Salt:

Description: This historic market in Salt's city center offers a glimpse into Jordan's past. Visitors can explore a range of shops selling textiles, spices, traditional clothing, and local products. It's a charming place to experience the authentic Jordanian market atmosphere.

Salt Town Center Mall:

Description: Located in the modern part of Salt, this mall features a mix of local and international stores, offering a variety of goods, including clothing, accessories, electronics, and more. It provides a contemporary shopping experience in the city.

JORDAN. VIBRANT NIGHTLIFE

Amman:

Clubs and Bars:

Amman boasts a thriving nightlife scene with a variety of bars and clubs. Places like Cube Lounge in Abdoun and Flip Jordan in Shmeisani offer a mix of music, dancing, and a lively atmosphere.

Rooftop Lounges:

Enjoy the cityscape at one of Amman's rooftop lounges. Oj's in Jabal Amman and Kudeta in Abdoun offer stunning views, live music, and a relaxed ambiance.

Cafes and Shisha Lounges:

For a more laid-back evening, explore the numerous cafes and shisha lounges in areas like Rainbow Street and Abdoun. These places offer a cozy atmosphere, local music, and a chance to mingle with locals and fellow travelers.

Aqaba:

Beachfront Bars:

Aqaba comes alive at night with beachfront bars and clubs. Tala Bay Resort and Captain's offer a mix of live music, dancing, and a chance to enjoy the Red Sea breeze.

Cafes by the Water:

Enjoy a more relaxed evening at cafes along the waterfront. Places like Rovers Return and Caffe Strada offer a perfect setting for a leisurely night out.

Irbid:

Local Hangouts:

Irbid's nightlife centers around local cafes and small bars. Places like Al-Murabaa'at and MIST Hookah Lounge offer a chance to experience the city's social scene.

Madaba:

Downtown Cafes:

Madaba's downtown area comes alive at night with cafes and restaurants. Cafe Haret Jdoudna offers a charming setting for an evening of relaxation and mingling.

Petra:

Bedouin Camps:

Experience a unique night in Petra by staying at a Bedouin camp. Many camps offer traditional music, stargazing, and a chance to connect with the local Bedouin culture.

Salt:

Local Hangouts:

Salt's nightlife revolves around local cafes and restaurants. Places like Shababeek Restaurant & Cafe offer a chance to enjoy a meal or a cup of coffee in a social setting.

10 AMAZING ITENERARIES IN JORDAN

Classic Jordan Exploration:

Duration: 7 Days

Highlights:

Day 1-2: Amman

Explore the historic downtown area, visit the Amman Citadel, and explore the Roman Theater.

Day 3-4: Petra

Discover the ancient city of Petra, including the iconic Treasury, Monastery, and hiking trails.

Day 5: Wadi Rum

Embark on a jeep tour in the stunning desert of Wadi Rum, experiencing Bedouin culture.

Day 6: Dead Sea

Float in the buoyant waters of the Dead Sea and indulge in spa treatments.

Day 7: Madaba and Mount Nebo

Visit St. George's Church in Madaba and enjoy panoramic views from Mount Nebo.

. Adventures in the South:

Duration: 5 Days

Highlights:

Day 1: Amman to Petra

Drive to Petra and explore the city's main attractions.

Day 2: Petra to Wadi Rum

Head to Wadi Rum for a day of desert adventures, including jeep tours and stargazing.

Day 3: Aqaba

Relax by the Red Sea, go snorkeling or diving, and explore the city's vibrant waterfront.

Day 4: Dana Biosphere Reserve

Hike through the beautiful landscapes of Dana and enjoy nature walks.

Day 5: Dead Sea

End your trip with a relaxing day at the Dead Sea.

. Historical Jordan Tour:

Duration: 8 Days

Highlights:

Day 1-3: Amman

Explore Amman's historical sites, including the Roman Theater, Citadel, and Archaeological Museum.

Day 4-5: Jerash and Ajloun

Visit the well-preserved Roman ruins of Jerash and explore the Ajloun Castle.

Day 6: Umm Qais

Discover the ancient Decapolis city of Umm Qais with its stunning views of the Sea of Galilee.

Day 7-8: Madaba, Mount Nebo, and Baptism Site

Explore Madaba's mosaics, visit Mount Nebo, and experience the Jordan River Baptism Site.

Desert Adventure:

Duration: 6 Days

Highlights:

Day 1-2: Amman to Dana Biosphere Reserve

Explore the diverse ecosystems of Dana, go on nature walks, and enjoy birdwatching.

Day 3: Little Petra and Wadi Araba

Visit the archaeological site of Little Petra before heading to the Wadi Araba Desert.

Day 4-6: Wadi Rum

Immerse yourself in the unique landscapes of Wadi Rum with jeep tours, rock climbing, and camping under the stars.

Cultural Immersion:

Duration: 10 Days

Highlights:

Day 1-3: Amman

Dive into Jordanian culture by exploring markets, enjoying local cuisine, and interacting with locals.

Day 4-6: Homestay in a Village

Experience traditional Jordanian life by staying with a local family in a village like Salt or Ajloun.

Day 7-10: Petra and Wadi Rum

Visit Petra and Wadi Rum while enjoying guided tours that provide insights into local culture and history.

Jordan's Northern Delights:

Duration: 6 Days

Highlights:

Day 1-2: Amman

Begin your journey in Amman, exploring its historical sites and vibrant markets.

Day 3: Jerash and Ajloun

Visit the ancient city of Jerash and explore the Ajloun Castle.

Day 4-5: Umm Qais and Pella

Discover the archaeological sites of Umm Qais and Pella in the northern Jordan Valley.

Day 6: Dead Sea

Relax at the Dead Sea and enjoy the therapeutic benefits of its mineral-rich waters.

Jordan's Religious Heritage:

Duration: 7 Days

Highlights:

Day 1-2: Amman

Begin your journey in Amman and explore religious sites such as the King Abdullah Mosque.

Day 3-4: Madaba, Mount Nebo, and Baptism Site

Visit St. George's Church, Mount Nebo, and the Jordan River Baptism Site.

Day 5: Umm Al-Jimal and Um Al-Qais

Explore the ancient sites of Umm Al-Jimal and Um Al-Qais, showcasing early Christian and Byzantine history.

Day 6-7: Petra

Discover the religious significance of Petra, including its early Christian and Nabatean sites.

Jordan's Culinary Adventure:

Duration: 8 Days

Highlights:

Day 1-2: Amman

Begin your culinary journey in Amman, exploring local markets and sampling authentic Jordanian dishes.

Day 3-4: Petra

Enjoy Petra's unique culinary offerings and explore local food markets.

Day 5: Wadi Rum

Experience traditional Bedouin cuisine in the heart of the desert.

Day 6-7: Aqaba

Savor fresh seafood and explore Aqaba's culinary scene along the Red Sea coast.

Day 8: Dead Sea

Indulge in spa treatments and savor gourmet meals with views of the Dead Sea.

Jordan's Nature and Adventure Tour:

Duration: 9 Days

Highlights:

Day 1-3: Dana Biosphere Reserve

Begin with nature walks and birdwatching in Dana, followed by a visit to Little Petra.

Day 4-6: Wadi Rum

Immerse yourself in the desert's unique landscapes with jeep tours, rock climbing, and camping.

Day 7-9: Aqaba and Underwater Adventures

Explore the Red Sea through snorkeling, diving, and water sports in Aqaba.

Jordan's Wellness Retreat:

Duration: 5 Days

Highlights:

Day 1-2: Dead Sea

Begin with relaxation and spa treatments at a luxury resort along the Dead Sea.

Day 3-4: Ma'in Hot Springs

Enjoy the therapeutic hot springs and waterfalls of Ma'in, surrounded by lush landscapes.

Day 5: Amman

Conclude your retreat with a visit to Amman's historical sites before departure.

IDEAL VISITING TIME

Spring (March to May):

Weather: Spring is one of the best times to visit Jordan. The temperatures are mild, ranging from comfortable daytime highs to cool evenings. The landscapes are lush, and wildflowers bloom, especially in areas like Dana Biosphere Reserve.

Highlights:

- Ideal for outdoor activities like hiking, exploring archaeological sites, and enjoying nature walks.
- Pleasant weather for visiting the Dead Sea, Wadi Rum, and Petra without extreme temperatures.

Events/Festivals:

- Amman International Theater Festival (April): A showcase of local and international theater productions.

Summer (June to August):

Weather: Summer in Jordan can be quite hot, particularly in areas like the Dead Sea and Aqaba, where temperatures can soar. However, in the highlands around Amman and Petra, the heat is more bearable.

Highlights:

- Ideal for water activities in the Red Sea, including snorkeling and diving.
- Nighttime stargazing in Wadi Rum, when the desert cools down.

Events/Festivals:

- Aqaba Summer Festival (July-August): Features cultural performances, music, and entertainment along the Red Sea coast.

Autumn (September to November):

Weather: Autumn is another excellent time to visit Jordan. The temperatures start to cool down, making it pleasant for outdoor activities. The landscapes remain beautiful, and the weather is generally comfortable.

Highlights:

- Great for exploring archaeological sites, including Petra and Jerash, with milder temperatures.

- Suitable for hiking in places like Dana Biosphere Reserve and Ajloun Forest Reserve.

Events/Festivals:

- Jerash Festival for Culture and Arts (July-September): A celebration of music, dance, and culture in the ancient city of Jerash.

Winter (December to February):

Weather: Winter in Jordan brings cooler temperatures, especially in the evenings. While the highlands can be chilly, the coastal areas like Aqaba and the Dead Sea remain relatively mild.

Highlights:

- Ideal for visiting historical sites like Madaba, Mount Nebo, and Um Qais.
- Possible to experience snowfall in places like Petra and the highlands near Amman.

Events/Festivals:

- Christmas and New Year's Celebrations: Jordan's Christian communities celebrate Christmas with special events and services.

JORDAN VOCABULARY AND COMMON PHRASE

Basic Phrases:

Hello:

- English: Hello
- Arabic: مرحبا (Marhaba)

Good morning:

- English: Good morning
- Arabic: صباح الخير (Sabah Al Khair)

Good afternoon/evening:

- English: Good afternoon/evening
- Arabic: مساء الخير (Masaa' Al Khair)

Goodbye:

- English: Goodbye
- Arabic: مع السلامة (Ma'a as-salama)

Thank you:

- English: Thank you
- Arabic: شكراً (Shukran)

You're welcome:

- English: You're welcome
- Arabic: اوفًا (Afwan)

Yes:

- English: Yes
- Arabic: نعم (Na'am)

No:

- English: No
- Arabic: لا (La)

Excuse me / Sorry:

- English: Excuse me / Sorry
- Arabic: ارذعً (A'zraan)

Please:

- English: Please
- Arabic: من فضلك (Min Fadlik)

I don't understand:

- English: I don't understand
- Arabic: لا أفهم (La Afham)

Where is...?:

- English: Where is...?
- Arabic: أين...؟ (Ayna...?)

How much is this?:

- English: How much is this?
- Arabic: بكم هذا؟ (Bikam Hatha?)

I would like...:

- English: I would like...
- Arabic: ...أريد (Uriid...)

Water:

- English: Water
- Arabic: ماء (Ma')

Food:

- English: Food
- Arabic: طعام (Ta'am)

Bathroom/Toilet:

- English: Bathroom/Toilet
- Arabic: حمام (Hammam)

Help:

- English: Help
- Arabic: مساعدة (Musa'ada)

Common Expressions:

Nice to meet you:

- English: Nice to meet you
- Arabic: بلقائك تشرفت (Tasharraftu biliqa'ik)

I'm lost:

- English: I'm lost
- Arabic: الطريق ضاعت (Da'at At-Tariq)

Can you help me, please?:

- English: Can you help me, please?
- Arabic: فضلك؟ من مساعدتي، يمكنك هل (Hal yumkinuka musa'adati, min fadlik?)

Where is the bus station?:

- English: Where is the bus station?
- Arabic: الحافلات؟ محطة أين (Ayna mahattat al-haafilat?)

I need a taxi:

- English: I need a taxi
- Arabic: أجرة سيارة أحتاج (Ahtaj sayyara ajra)

I want to go to...:

- English: I want to go to...

- Arabic: إلى...أريد أن أذهب (Uriidu an adhaba ila...)

Do you speak English?:

- English: Do you speak English?
- Arabic: الإنجليزية؟ تتحدث هل (Hal tatahaddath al-ingliziya?)

I'm a tourist:

- English: I'm a tourist
- Arabic: سائح أنا (Ana sayyih)

Can I have the bill, please?:

- English: Can I have the bill, please?
- Arabic: فضلك؟ من الفاتورة على الحصول يمكنني هل (Hal yumkinuni al-husul 'ala al-fatuura min fadlik?)

I love Jordan!:

- English: I love Jordan!
- Arabic: الأردن أحب أنا! (Ana uhibb al-Urdun!)

Can you recommend a good restaurant?:

- English: Can you recommend a good restaurant?
- Arabic: جيد؟ بمطعم توصي أن يمكنك هل (Hal yumkinuka an tawsii bi-maT'am jayyid?)

What time is it?:

- English: What time is it?
- Arabic: كم الساعة؟ (Kam as-saa'a?)

I'm not feeling well:

- English: I'm not feeling well
- Arabic: لا أشعر بتحسن (La ash'ur bitaHsin)

Can I use the internet here?:

- English: Can I use the internet here?
- Arabic: هل يمكنني استخدام الإنترنت هنا؟ (Hal yumkinuni istikhdam al-internet huna?)

Where can I buy souvenirs?:

- English: Where can I buy souvenirs?
- Arabic: أين يمكنني شراء الهدايا التذكارية؟ (Ayna yumkinuni shira' al-hadiyat at-tadhkariya?)

I'm lost. Can you help me find my way back to the hotel?:

- English: I'm lost. Can you help me find my way back to the hotel?
- Arabic: ضاعت الطريق. هل يمكنك مساعدتي في العثور على الطريق إلى الفندق؟ (Da'at at-tariq. Hal yumkinuka musa'adati fi al-'uthur 'ala at-tariq ila al-funduq?)

Can I have a menu, please?:

- English: Can I have a menu, please?
- Arabic: هل يمكنني الحصول على القائمة من فضلك؟ (Hal yumkinuni al-husul 'ala al-qa'imah min fadlik?)

I'm vegetarian:

- English: I'm vegetarian
- Arabic: أنا نباتي (Ana nabati)

I don't eat pork:

- English: I don't eat pork
- Arabic: أنا لا أكل لحم الخنزير (Ana la aakulu lahmu al-khinzir)

How much is the entrance fee?:

- English: How much is the entrance fee?
- Arabic: كم سعر تذكرة الدخول؟ (Kam sa'r tazkirat ad-dukhul?)

Numbers:

- 1: واحد (waahid)
- 2: اثنان (ithnaan)
- 3: ثلاثة (thalaatha)
- 4: أربعة (arba'a)

- 5: خمسة (khamsa)
- 6: ستة (sitta)
- 7: سبعة (sab'a)
- 8: ثمانية (thamaaniya)
- 9: تسعة (tis'a)
- 10: عشرة (ashara)

TRAVELING PRACTICALITIES

Visa and Entry Requirements:

Visa: Most travelers to Jordan require a visa to enter the country. Visas can be obtained upon arrival at the airport or land borders, or in advance from Jordanian embassies or consulates. It's advisable to check the specific requirements based on your nationality before traveling.

Visa Fees: The visa fee varies depending on the length of stay and nationality. It's recommended to carry cash (in Jordanian Dinars or USD) for visa fees, as credit cards may not always be accepted.

Currency and Payment Methods:

Currency: The official currency of Jordan is the Jordanian Dinar (JOD). It's recommended to carry a mix of cash and credit/debit cards.

ATMs and Banks: ATMs are widely available in cities and towns. Major credit and debit cards are accepted in most establishments, but it's advisable to carry some cash for smaller vendors and in more remote areas.

Language:

Official Language: Arabic is the official language of Jordan.

English: English is widely spoken, especially in tourist areas, hotels, and restaurants. Many signs are also in English.

Transportation:

Public Transport: Jordan has a well-developed public transportation system, including buses and shared taxis (known as "service taxis"). They are affordable and can take you between cities and within urban areas.

Private Taxis: Taxis are readily available in cities. Ensure the meter is used, or negotiate a fare before starting the journey.

Rental Cars: Renting a car provides flexibility, especially if you plan to explore more remote areas. International and local car rental agencies operate in Jordan.

Petra Shuttle: In Petra, there is a convenient shuttle service that transports visitors from the entrance to various sites within Petra Archaeological Park.

Accommodation:

Types of Accommodation: Jordan offers a range of accommodation options including hotels, guesthouses, hostels, and Bedouin camps. It's recommended to book in advance, especially during peak tourist seasons.

Popular Areas to Stay:

Amman: Areas like Abdoun, Jabal Amman, and Downtown are popular for accommodation.

Petra: Wadi Musa is the town nearest to Petra, offering a variety of hotels and guesthouses.

Aqaba: The city center and beachfront areas have a range of accommodation options.

Health and Safety:

Health Precautions: It's advisable to have up-to-date vaccinations and consult a healthcare provider for any necessary travel vaccinations before visiting Jordan.

Travel Insurance: It's highly recommended to have travel insurance that covers medical emergencies, trip cancellations, and other unforeseen events.

Safety: Jordan is considered relatively safe for travelers. However, it's always important to be aware of your surroundings and follow any local advice or guidelines.

Communication:

SIM Cards: Local SIM cards are readily available for purchase, providing affordable data and call options. Major cities and tourist areas have good network coverage.

Internet Access: Wi-Fi is widely available in hotels, cafes, and public spaces.

Remember to check for any travel advisories or specific requirements related to your nationality before visiting Jordan.

CONCLUSION

In the pages of "Jordan Travel Guide 2024 Updated," you've embarked on a journey through the enchanting landscapes and rich cultural tapestry of this remarkable country. From the ancient ruins of Petra to the sweeping dunes of Wadi Rum, you've uncovered hidden treasures that have left an indelible mark on your soul.

As you've explored the vibrant markets of Amman, tasted the savory delights of Jordanian cuisine, and witnessed the warm hospitality of its people, you've become not just a traveler, but a cherished guest in this land of wonders.

This guide, filled with insights and practical tips, has been your trusty companion, illuminating the path to unforgettable experiences and opening doors to authentic encounters. Whether you've wandered through the bustling streets of Amman, hiked the rugged trails of Dana Biosphere Reserve, or marveled at the star-studded skies over Wadi Rum, each moment has been a testament to the enduring allure of Jordan.

As you close the final chapter, remember that your journey doesn't end here. The memories you've created will forever linger in your heart, beckoning you back to the timeless beauty of Jordan. And should you ever return, the treasures of this land will welcome you with open arms, ready to unveil new adventures and stories.

With deepest gratitude, we thank you for allowing us to be a part of your journey. May the spirit of Jordan stay with you, guiding your travels and filling your heart with the magic of this extraordinary land. Until we meet again, happy travels!

[Harrison wells]

Made in the USA
Las Vegas, NV
14 December 2023

82776346R00079